Sam Harris

Lying

FOUR ELEPHANTS PRESS

Four Elephants Press

All rights reserved. Published in the United States by
Four Elephants Press.

Library of Congress Cataloging-in-Publication Data
Harris, Sam, date.
Lying / Sam Harris.—1st ed.
p. cm.
Library of Congress Control Number: 2013947127

ISBN 978-1-9400-5100-0
1. Ethics. 2. Values. 3. Lying and deception. I. Title.

10   9

For Emma

Among the many paradoxes of human life, this is perhaps the most peculiar and consequential: *We often behave in ways that are guaranteed to make us unhappy.* Many of us spend our lives marching with open eyes toward remorse, regret, guilt, and disappointment. And nowhere do our injuries seem more casually self-inflicted, or the suffering we create more disproportionate to the needs of the moment, than in the lies we tell to other human beings. Lying is the royal road to chaos.

As an undergraduate at Stanford, I took a seminar that profoundly changed my life. It was called "The Ethical Analyst," and it was conducted in the form of a Socratic dialogue by an extraordinarily gifted professor, Ronald A. Howard.[1] Our discussion focused on a single question of practical ethics:

Is it wrong to lie?

At first glance, this may seem a scant foundation for an entire college course. After all, most people already believe that lying is generally wrong—and they also know that some situations seem to warrant it. What was so fascinating about this seminar, however, was how difficult it was to find examples of virtuous lies that could withstand Professor Howard's scrutiny. Whatever the circumstances, even in cases where most good people would lie without a qualm, Howard nearly always found truths worth telling.

I do not remember what I thought about lying before I took "The Ethical Analyst," but the course accomplished as close to a firmware upgrade of my brain as I have ever experienced. I came away convinced that lying, even about the smallest matters, needlessly damages personal relationships and public trust.

It would be hard to exaggerate what a relief it was to realize this. It's not that I had been in the habit of lying before taking Howard's course—but I now knew that endless forms of suffering and embarrassment could be easily avoided by *simply telling the truth*. And, as though for the first time, I saw all around me the consequences of others' failure to live by this principle.

That experience remains one of the clearest examples in my life of the power of philosophical reflection. "The

Ethical Analyst" affected me in ways that college courses seldom do: It made me a better person.

What Is a Lie?

Deception can take many forms, but not all acts of deception are lies. Even the most ethical among us regularly struggle to keep appearances and reality apart. By wearing cosmetics, a woman seeks to seem younger or more beautiful than she otherwise would. But honesty does not require that she issue continual disclaimers—"I see that you are looking at my face: Please be aware that I do not look this good first thing in the morning . . ." A person in a hurry might pretend not to notice an acquaintance passing by on the street. A polite host might not acknowledge that one of her guests has said something so stupid as to slow the rotation of the earth. When asked "How are you?" most of us reflexively say that we are well, understanding the question to be merely a greeting, rather than an invitation to discuss our career disappointments, our marital troubles, or the condition of our bowels. Elisions of this kind can be forms of deception, but they are not quite lies. We may skirt the truth at such moments, but we do not deliberately manufacture falsehood or conceal important facts to the detriment of others.

The boundary between lying and deception is often vague. It is even possible to deceive with the truth. I could, for instance, stand on the sidewalk in front of the White House and call the headquarters of Facebook on my cell phone: "Hello, this is Sam Harris. I'm calling from the White House, and I'd like to speak to Mark Zuckerberg." My words would, in a narrow sense, be true—but the statement seems calculated to deceive. Would I be lying? Close enough.

To lie is to intentionally mislead others when they expect honest communication.[2] This leaves stage magicians, poker players, and other harmless dissemblers off the hook, while illuminating a psychological and social landscape whose general shape is very easy to recognize. People lie so that others will form beliefs that are not true. The more consequential the beliefs—that is, the more a person's well-being demands a correct understanding of the world or of other people's opinions—the more consequential the lie.

As the philosopher Sissela Bok observed, however, we cannot get far on this topic without first distinguishing between truth and truthfulness—for a person may be impeccably truthful while being mistaken.[3] To speak truthfully is to accurately represent one's beliefs. But candor offers no assurance that one's beliefs about the world are true. Nor does truthfulness require that one speak the *whole* truth, because communicating every fact on a given topic is almost never useful or even possible. Of course, if one is not sure whether or not something is true, representing one's degree of uncertainty is a form of honesty.

Leaving these ambiguities aside, communicating what one believes to be both true and useful is surely different from concealing or distorting that belief. The *intent* to communicate honestly is the measure of truthfulness. And most of us do not require a degree in philosophy to distinguish this attitude from its counterfeits.

People tell lies for many reasons. They lie to avoid embarrassment, to exaggerate their accomplishments, and to disguise wrongdoing. They make promises they do not intend to keep. They conceal defects in their products or services. They mislead competitors to gain advantage. Many of us lie to our friends and family members to spare their feelings.

Whatever our purpose in telling them, lies can be gross or subtle. Some entail elaborate ruses or forged documents. Others consist merely of euphemisms or tactical silences. But it is in believing one thing while intending to communicate another that every lie is born.

We have all stood on both sides of the divide between what someone believes and what he intends others to understand—and the gap generally looks quite different depending on whether one is the liar or the dupe. The liar often imagines that he does no harm so long as his lies go undetected. But the one lied to rarely shares this view. The moment we consider our dishonesty from the perspective of those we lie to, we recognize that we would feel betrayed if the roles were reversed.

A friend of mine, Sita, was once going to visit the home of another friend and wanted to take her a small gift. Unfortunately, she was traveling with her young son and hadn't found time to go shopping. As they were getting ready to leave their hotel, however, Sita noticed that the bath products supplied in their room were unusually nice. So she put some soaps, shampoos, and body lotions into a bag, tied it with a ribbon she got at the front desk, and set off.

When Sita presented this gift, her friend was delighted.

"Where did you get them?" she asked.

Surprised by the question, and by a lurching sense of impropriety, Sita sought to regain her footing with a lie: "Oh, we just bought them in the hotel gift shop."

The next words came from her innocent son: "No, Mommy, you got them in the bathroom!"

Imagine the faces of these women, briefly frozen in embarrassment and then yielding to smiles of apology and forgiveness. This may seem the most trivial of lies—and it was—but it surely did nothing to increase the level of trust between two friends. Funny or not, the story reveals something distasteful about Sita: She will lie when it suits her needs.

The opportunity to deceive others is ever present and often tempting, and each instance of deception casts us onto some of the steepest ethical terrain we ever cross. Few of us are murderers or thieves, but we have all been liars. And many of us will be unable to get into our beds tonight without having told several lies over the course of the day.

What does this say about us and about the life we are making with one another?

The Mirror of Honesty

At least one study suggests that 10 percent of communication between spouses is deceptive.[4] Another found that 38 percent of encounters among college students contain lies.[5] Lying is ubiquitous, and yet even liars rate their deceptive interactions as less pleasant than truthful ones. This is not terribly surprising: We know that trust is deeply rewarding and that deception and suspicion are two sides of the same coin. Research suggests that all forms of lying—including white lies meant to spare the feelings of others—are associated with less satisfying relationships.[6]

Once one commits to telling the truth, one begins to notice how unusual it is to meet someone who shares this commitment. Honest people are a refuge: You know they mean what they say; you know they will not say one thing to your face and another behind your back; you know they will tell you when they think you have failed—and for this reason their praise cannot be mistaken for mere flattery.

Honesty is a gift we can give to others. It is also a source of power and an engine of simplicity. Knowing that we will attempt to tell the truth, whatever the circumstances, leaves us with little to prepare for. Knowing that we told the truth in the past leaves us with nothing to keep track of. We can simply be ourselves in every moment.

In committing to being honest with everyone, we commit to avoiding a wide range of long-term problems, but at the cost of occasional short-term discomfort. However, the discomfort should not be exaggerated: You can be honest and kind, because your purpose in telling the truth is not to offend people. You simply want them to have the information you have and would want to have if you were in their shoes.

But it may take practice to feel comfortable with this way of being in the world—to cancel plans, decline invitations, negotiate contracts, critique others' work, all while being honest about what one is thinking and feeling. To do this is also to hold a mirror up to one's life—because a commitment to telling the truth requires that one pay attention to what the truth is in every moment. What sort of person are you? How judgmental, self-interested, or petty have you become?

You might discover that some of your friendships are not really that—perhaps you habitually lie to avoid making plans, or fail to express your true opinions for fear of conflict. Whom, exactly, are you helping by living this way? You might find that certain relationships cannot be honestly maintained. Of course, we all have associations that must persist in some form, whether we enjoy them or not—with family, in-laws, colleagues, employers, and so forth. I'm not denying that tact can play a role in minimizing conflict. Holding one's tongue, or steering a conversation toward topics of relative safety, is not the same as lying (nor does it require that one deny the truth in the future).

Honesty can force any dysfunction in your life to the surface. Are you in an abusive relationship? A refusal to lie to others—How did you get that bruise?—would oblige you to come to grips with this situation very quickly. Do you have a problem with drugs or alcohol? Lying is the lifeblood of addiction. If we have no recourse to lies, our lives can unravel only so far without others' noticing.

Telling the truth can also reveal ways in which we want to grow but haven't. I remember learning that I had been selected as the class valedictorian at my high school. I declined the honor, saying that I felt that someone who had been at the school longer should give the graduation speech. But that was a lie. The truth was that I was terrified of public speaking and would do almost anything to avoid it. Apparently, I wasn't ready to confront this fact about myself—and my willingness to lie at that moment allowed me to avoid doing so for many years. Had I been forced to tell my high school principal the truth, he might have begun a conversation with me that would have been well worth having.

Two Types of Lies

Ethical transgressions are generally divided into two categories: the bad things we do (acts of commission) and the good things we fail to do (acts of omission). We tend to judge the former far more harshly. The origin of this imbalance is somewhat mysterious, but it surely relates to the value we place on a person's energy and intent. *Doing* something requires energy, and most morally salient actions are associated with conscious intent. *Failing to do* something can arise purely by circumstance and requires energy to rectify. The difference is important. It is one thing to reach into the till and steal $100; it is another to neglect to return $100 that one has received by mistake. We might consider both behaviors to be ethically blameworthy—but only the former amounts to a deliberate effort to steal. Needless to say, if it would cost a person *more* than $100 to return $100 he received by mistake, few of us would judge him for simply keeping the money.[7]

And so it is with lying. To lie about one's age, marital status, or career is one thing; to fail to correct false impressions whenever they arise is another. For instance, I am occasionally described as a "neurologist," which I am not, rather than as a "neuroscientist." Neurologists have medical degrees and specialize in treating disorders of the brain and nervous system. Neuroscientists have PhDs and perform research. I am not an MD, have no clinical experience, and would never dream of claiming to be a neurologist. But neither do I view it as my ethical responsibility to correct every instance of confusion that might arise on this point. (A Google search for "Sam Harris" and "neurologist" suggests that it would simply take too much energy.) If, however, a person's belief that I am a neurologist ever seemed likely to cause harm, or to redound to my advantage, I would be guilty of a lie of omission, and it would be ethically important for me to clear the matter up. And yet few people would view my failure to do so as equivalent to my falsely claiming to be a neurologist in the first place.

In discussing the phenomenon of lying, I will generally focus on lies of commission: lying at its clearest and most consequential. However, most of what I say is relevant to lies of omission and to deception generally. I will also focus on "white" lies—those lies we tell for the purpose of sparing others discomfort—for they are the lies that most often tempt us. And they tend to be the only lies that good people tell while imagining that they are being good in the process.

White Lies

Have you ever received a truly awful gift? The time it took to tear away the wrapping paper should have allowed you to steel yourself—but suddenly there it was:

"Wow . . ."

"Do you like it?"

"That's amazing. Where did you get it?"

"Bangkok. Do you like it?"

"When were you in Bangkok?"

"Christmas. Do you like it?"

"Yes . . . Definitely. Where else did you go in Thailand?"

I have now broken into a cold sweat. I am not cut out for this. Generally speaking, I have learned to be honest even when ambushed. I don't always communicate the truth in the way that I want to—but one of the strengths of telling the truth is that it remains open for elaboration. If what you say in the heat of the moment isn't quite right, you can amend it. I have learned that I would rather be maladroit, or even rude, than dishonest.

What could I have said in the above situation?

"Wow . . . Does one wear it or hang it on the wall?"

"You wear it. It's very warm. Do you like it?"

"You know, I'm really touched you thought of me. But there's no way I can pull this off. My style is somewhere between boring and very boring."

This is getting much closer to the sort of response I'm comfortable with. Some euphemism is creeping in, perhaps, but the basic communication is truthful. I have given my friend fair warning that she is unlikely to see me wearing her gift the next time we meet. I have also given her an opportunity to keep it for herself or perhaps bestow it on another friend who might actually like it.

Some readers may now worry that I am recommending a regression to the social ineptitude of early childhood. After all, children do not learn to tell white lies until about the age of four, once they have achieved a hard-won awareness of the mental states of others.[8] But we have no reason to believe that the social conventions that happen to stabilize in primates like ourselves at about the age of eleven will lead to optimal human relationships. In fact, there are many reasons to believe that lying is precisely the sort of behavior we need to outgrow in order to build a better world.

What could be wrong with truly "white" lies? First, they are still lies. And in telling them, we incur all the problems of being less than straightforward in our dealings with other people. Sincerity, authenticity, integrity, mutual understanding—these and other sources of moral wealth are destroyed the moment we deliberately misrepresent our beliefs, whether or not our lies are ever discovered.

And although we imagine that we tell certain lies out of compassion for others, it is rarely difficult to spot the damage we do in the process. By lying, we deny our friends access to reality[9]—and their resulting ignorance often harms them in ways we did not anticipate. Our friends may act on our falsehoods, or fail to solve problems that could have been solved only on the basis of good information. Rather often, to lie is to infringe on the freedom of those we care about.

A primal instance:

"Do I look fat in this dress?"

Most people insist that the correct answer to this question is always "No." In fact, many believe that it's not a question at all: The woman is simply saying, "Tell me I look good." If she's your wife or girlfriend, she might even be saying, "Tell me you love me." If you sincerely believe that this is the situation you are in— that the text is a distraction and the subtext conveys the entire message—then so be it. Responding honestly to the subtext would not be lying.

But this is an edge case for a reason: It crystallizes what is tempting about white lies. Why not simply reassure someone with a tiny lie and send her out into the world feeling more confident? Unless one commits to telling the truth in situations like this, however, one finds that the edges creep inward, and exceptions to the principle of honesty begin to multiply. Very soon, you may find yourself behaving as most people do quite effortlessly: shading the truth, or even lying outright, without thinking about it. The price is too high.

A friend of mine recently asked me whether I thought he was overweight. In fact he probably was just asking for reassurance: It was the beginning of summer, and we were sitting with our wives by the side of his pool. However, I'm more comfortable relying on the words that actually come out of a person's mouth, rather than on my powers of telepathy. So I answered my friend's question very directly: "No one would ever call you 'fat,' but if I were you, I'd want to lose twenty-five pounds." That was two months ago, and he is now fifteen pounds lighter.[10] Neither of us knew that he was ready to go on a diet until I declined the opportunity to lie about how he looked in a bathing suit.

Back to our friend in the dress: What is the truth? Perhaps she does look fat in that dress but it's the fault of the dress. Telling her the truth will allow her to find a more flattering outfit.

But let's imagine the truth is harder to tell: Your friend looks fat in that dress, or any dress, because she *is* fat. Let's say she is also thirty-five years old and single, and you know that her greatest desire is to get married and start a family. You also believe that many men would be disinclined to date her at her current weight.

And, marriage aside, you are confident that she would be happier and healthier, and would feel better about herself, if she got in shape.

A white lie is simply a denial of these realities. It is a refusal to offer honest guidance in a storm. Even on so touchy a subject, lying seems a clear failure of friendship. By reassuring your friend about her appearance, you are not helping her to do what you think she should do to get what she wants out of life.[11]

In many circumstances in life, false encouragement can be very costly to another person. Imagine that you have a friend who has spent years striving unsuccessfully to build a career as an actor. Many fine actors struggle in this way, of course, but in your friend's case the reason seems self-evident: He is a terrible actor. In fact, you know that his other friends—and even his parents—share this opinion but cannot bring themselves to express it. What do you say the next time he complains about his stalled career? Do you encourage him to "just keep at it"? False encouragement is a kind of theft: It steals time, energy, and motivation that a person could put toward some other purpose.

This is not to say that we are always correct in our judgments of other people. And honesty demands that we communicate any uncertainty we may feel about the relevance of our own opinions. But if we are convinced that a friend has taken a wrong turn in life, it is no sign of friendship to simply smile and wave him onward.

If the truth itself is painful to tell, often background truths are not—and these can be communicated as well, deepening the friendship. In the examples above, the more basic truth is that you love your friends and want them to be happy, and they could make changes in their lives that might lead to greater fulfillment. In lying to them, you are not only declining to help them—you are denying them useful information and setting them up for future disappointment. Yet the temptation to lie in these circumstances can be overwhelming.

When we presume to lie for the benefit of others, we have decided that *we* are the best judges of how much they should understand about their own lives—about how they appear, their reputations, or their prospects in the world. This is an extraordinary stance to adopt toward other human beings, and it requires justification. Unless someone is suicidal or otherwise on the brink, deciding how much he should know about himself seems the quintessence of arrogance. What attitude could be more disrespectful of those we care about?

While preparing to write this book, I asked friends and readers for examples of lies that had affected them.

Some of their stories appear below. (I have changed all names to protect the innocent and the guilty alike.)

Many people talked about family members who had deceived one another about medical diagnoses. Here is one example:

> My mother was diagnosed with MS when she was in her late 30s. Her doctor thought it was best to lie and tell her that she didn't have MS. He told my father the truth. My father decided to keep the truth to himself because he didn't want to upset my mother or any of their 3 children.
>
> Meanwhile, my mother went to the library, read up on her symptoms, and diagnosed herself with MS. She decided not to tell my father or their children because she didn't want to upset anyone.
>
> One year later, when she went to the doctor for her annual checkup, the doctor told her she had MS. She confessed that she knew but hadn't told anyone. My dad confessed that he knew but hadn't told anyone. So they each spent a year with a secret and without each other's support.
>
> My brother found out accidentally about a year later, when my mother had breast cancer surgery. The surgeon walked into the room and essentially said, "This won't affect the MS." My brother said, "What

MS?" I think it was a couple more years before anyone told me or my sister about Mom's MS. . . . Rather than feeling grateful and protected, I felt sadness that we hadn't come together as a family to face her illness and support each other.

My mother never told her mother about the MS, which meant that none of us could tell friends and family, for fear that her mother would find out. She didn't want to hurt her mother. I think she deprived herself of the opportunity to have a closer relationship with her mother.

Such instances of medical deception were once extraordinarily common. In fact, I know of at least one within my own family: My maternal grandmother died of cancer when my mother was sixteen. She had been suffering from metastatic melanoma for nearly a year, but her doctor had told her that she had arthritis. Her husband, my grandfather, knew her actual diagnosis but decided to maintain the deception as well.

After my grandmother's condition deteriorated, and she was finally hospitalized, she confided to a nurse that she knew she was dying. However, she imagined that she had been keeping this a secret from the rest of her family, her husband included. My mother and her younger brother were kept entirely in the dark. In their experience, their mother checked in to the hospital for "arthritis" and never returned.

Think of all the opportunities for deepening love, compassion, forgiveness, and understanding that are forsaken by white lies of this kind. When we pretend not to know the truth, we must also pretend not to be motivated by it. This can force us to make choices that we would not otherwise make. Did my grandfather really have *nothing* to say to his wife in light of the fact that she would soon die? Did she really have *nothing* to say to her two children to help prepare them for their lives without her? These silences are lacerating. Wisdom remains unshared, promises unmade, and apologies unoffered. The opportunity to say something useful to the people we love soon disappears, never to return.

Who would choose to leave this world in such terrible isolation? Perhaps there are those who would. But why should anyone make the choice for another person?

Trust

Jessica recently overheard her friend Lucy telling a white lie: Lucy had a social obligation she wanted to get free of, and Jessica heard her leave a voicemail message for another friend, explaining why their meeting would have to be rescheduled. Lucy's excuse was entirely fictitious—something involving her child's being sick—but she lied so effortlessly and persuasively that Jessica was left wondering if she had ever been deceived by Lucy in the past. Now, whenever Lucy cancels a plan, Jessica suspects she might not be telling the truth.

Such tiny erosions of trust are especially insidious because they are almost never remedied. Lucy has no reason to think that Jessica has a grievance against her—because she doesn't. She simply does not trust her as much as she used to, having heard her lie without compunction to another friend. Of course, if the problem (or the relationship) were deeper, perhaps Jessica would say something—but as it happens, she feels there is no point in admonishing Lucy about her ethics. The net result is that a single voicemail message, left for a third party, has subtly undermined a friendship.

We have already seen that children can be dangerous to keep around if one wants to lie with impunity. Another example, in case there is any doubt: My friend Daniel recently learned from his wife that another couple would be coming to stay in their home for a week. Daniel resisted. A week seemed like an eternity—especially given that he was not at all fond of the husband. This precipitated a brief argument between Daniel and his wife in the presence of their young daughter.

In the end, Daniel gave in, and the couple was soon standing on his doorstep with an impressive amount of luggage. Upon entering the home, the unwelcome husband expressed his gratitude for being allowed to stay in Daniel's guest room.

"Don't be silly, it's great to see you," Daniel said, his daughter standing at his side. "We love having you here."

"But Dad, you said you didn't want them to stay with us."

"No I didn't."

"Yes you did! Remember?"

"No, no . . . that was another situation." Daniel found that he could no longer maintain eye contact with his guests and thought of nothing better than to lead his daughter away by the hand, saying, "Where is your coloring book?"

There is comedy here—but only for others. And what do our children learn about us in moments like these? Is this really the example we want to set for them? Failures of personal integrity, once revealed, are rarely forgotten. We can apologize, of course. And we can resolve to be more forthright in the future. But we cannot erase the bad impression we have left in the minds of other people.

Again, I am not denying that tact has a place in encounters of this kind. If Daniel had said, "That's what guest rooms are for . . . How was your trip?" he would have finessed the issue without starkly misrepresenting his feelings in front of his daughter. Communications like these can still be awkward, but a wasteland of embarrassment and social upheaval can generally be avoided by following a single precept: *Do not lie.*

Faint Praise

There have been times in my life when I was devoted to a project that was simply doomed, in which I had months—in one case, *years*—invested, and when honest feedback could have spared me an immense amount of wasted effort. At other times, I received frank criticism just when I needed it and was able to change course quickly, knowing that I had avoided a lot of painful and unnecessary work. The difference between these two fates is hard to exaggerate. Yes, it can be unpleasant to be told that we have wasted time, or that we are not performing as well as we imagined, but if the criticism is valid, it is precisely what we most need to hear to find our way in the world.

And yet we are often tempted to encourage others with insincere praise. In this we treat them like children—while failing to help them prepare for encounters with those who will judge them like adults. I'm not saying that we need to go out of our way to criticize others. But when asked for an honest opinion, we do our friends no favors by pretending not to notice flaws in their work, especially when those who are not their friends are bound to notice the same flaws. Sparing others disappointment and embarrassment is a great kindness. And if we have a history of being honest, our praise and encouragement will actually mean something.

I have a friend who is a very successful writer. Early in his career, he wrote a script that I thought was terrible, and I told him so. That was not easy to do, because he had spent the better part of a year working on it—but it was the truth (as I saw it). Now, when I tell him that I love something he has written, he knows that I love it. He also knows that I respect his talent enough to tell him when I don't. I am sure there are people in his life he can't say that about. Why would I want to be one of them?

Secrets

A commitment to honesty does not necessarily require that we disclose facts about ourselves that we would prefer to keep private. If someone asks how much money you have in your bank account, you are under no ethical obligation to tell him. The truth could well be "I'd rather not say."

So there is no conflict, in principle, between honesty and the keeping of secrets. However, it is worth noting that many secrets—especially those we are asked to keep for others—can put us in a position where we will be forced to choose between lying and revealing privileged information. To agree to keep a secret is to assume a burden. At a minimum, one must remember what one is not supposed to talk about. This can be difficult and lead to clumsy attempts at deception. Unless your work requires that you keep secrets—which doctors, lawyers, psychologists, and other professional confidants do routinely—it seems worth avoiding.

Stephanie and Gina had been friends for more than a decade when Stephanie began to hear rumors that Gina's husband, Derek, was having an affair. Although Stephanie did not feel close enough to Gina to raise the matter directly, a little snooping revealed that almost everyone in her circle knew about Derek's infidelity— except, it seemed, Gina herself.

Derek had not been discreet. He was in the film business, and his mistress was an aspiring actress. Once, while traveling with Gina and the kids on vacation, he had booked this woman a room in the same hotel. He later hired her as a production assistant, and she now accompanied him on business trips and even attended events where Gina was present.

As Gina's friend, Stephanie wanted to do whatever she could to help her. But what was the right thing to do? She was a second-tier friend, and the person who had told her of Derek's affair had sworn her to secrecy. She also knew women who were closer to Gina than she was—why hadn't one of them said something?

Stephanie saw Gina a few more times—they had been having lunch regularly for years—but found that she could no longer enjoy her company. Gina would speak about the completion of her new home, or about plans for an upcoming trip, and Stephanie would feel that by remaining silent she was participating in her friend's ultimate undoing. Simply having a normal conversation became an ordeal of acting as if nothing were the matter. Whether Gina knew about her husband's behavior and was keeping it a secret, was self-deceived, or was merely a victim of his cunning and the collusion of others, Stephanie's pretense began to feel indistinguishable from lying. As if by magic, the two friends quickly grew apart and have not spoken for years.

Stephanie knew several people with direct knowledge of Derek's philandering who quietly severed their relationships with him—all while keeping Gina in the dark (or allowing her to keep herself there). She found it uncanny to see someone living under a mountain of lies and gossip, surrounded by friends but without a friend in the world who would tell her the truth. And this was Derek's final victory: People who could no longer abide him because of his unconscionable treatment of his wife nevertheless helped maintain his lies—and abandoned his wife in the process.

Lies in Extremis

Kant believed that lying was unethical in all cases—even in an attempt to stop the murder of an innocent person. As with many of Kant's philosophical views, his position on lying was not so much argued for as presumed, like a religious precept. Though *Never tell a lie* has the obvious virtue of clarity, in practice this rule can produce behavior that only a psychopath might endorse.

A total prohibition against lying is also ethically incoherent in anyone but a true pacifist. If you think that it can ever be appropriate to injure or kill a person in self-defense, or in defense of another, it makes no sense to rule out lying in the same circumstances.[12]

I cannot see any reason to take Kant seriously on this point—which does not mean that lying is easily justified. Even as a means to ward off violence, lying often closes the door to acts of honest communication that might be more effective or produce important moral breakthroughs.

In those circumstances where we deem it *obviously* necessary to lie, we have generally determined that the person to be deceived is both dangerous and unreachable by any recourse to the truth. In other words, we have judged the prospects of establishing a genuine relationship with him to be nonexistent. For most of us, such circumstances arise very rarely in life, if ever. And even when they seem to, it is often possible to worry that lying was the easy (and less than perfectly ethical) way out.

Let us take an extreme case as a template for others in the genre: A known murderer is looking for a boy whom you are now sheltering in your home. The murderer is standing at your door and wants to know whether you have seen his intended victim. The temptation to lie is perfectly understandable—but merely lying might produce other outcomes you do not intend. If you say that you saw the boy climb your fence and continue down the block, the murderer may leave, only to kill someone else's child. Even in this unhappy case, lying might have been your best hope for protecting innocent life. But that doesn't mean someone more courageous or capable than you couldn't have produced a better result with the truth.

Telling the truth in such a circumstance need not amount to acquiescence. The truth in this case could well be "I wouldn't tell you even if I knew. And if you take another step, I'll put a bullet in your head." If lying seems the only option, given your fear or physical limitations, it clearly shifts the burden of combating evil onto others. Granted, your neighbors might be better able to assume this burden than you are. But *someone* must assume it eventually. If no one else, the police must tell murderers the truth: Their behavior will not be tolerated.

It is far more common to find ourselves in situations in which, though we are tempted to lie, honesty will lead us to form connections with people who might other- wise have been adversaries. In this vein, I recall an encounter I had with a U.S. Customs officer upon returning from my first trip to Asia.

The year was 1987, but it might as well have been the Summer of Love: I was twenty, had hair down to my shoulders, and was dressed like an Indian rickshaw driver. For those charged with enforcing our nation's drug laws, it would have been only prudent to subject my luggage to special scrutiny. Happily, I had nothing to hide.

"Where are you coming from?" the officer asked, glancing skeptically at my backpack.

"India, Nepal, Thailand . . ." I said.

"Did you take any drugs while you were over there?"

As it happens, I had. The temptation to lie was obvious—why speak to a *Customs officer* about my recent drug use? But I had no real reason not to tell the truth, apart from the risk that it would lead to an even more thorough search of my luggage (and perhaps of my person) than had already commenced.

"Yes," I said.

The officer stopped searching my bag and looked up. "Which ones did you take?

"I smoked pot a few times . . . And I tried opium in India."

"Opium?"

"Yes."

"Opium or heroin?

"It was opium."

"You don't hear much about opium these days."

"I know. It was the first time I'd ever tried it."

"Are you carrying any drugs with you now?"

"No."

The officer eyed me warily for a moment and then returned to searching my bag. Given the nature of our conversation, I reconciled myself to being there for a very long time. I was, therefore, as patient as a tree. Which was a good thing, because the officer was now examining my belongings as though any one item—a toothbrush, a book, a flashlight, a bit of nylon cord—might reveal the deepest secrets of the universe.

"What is opium like?" he asked after a time.

I told him. In fact, over the next ten minutes, I told this lawman almost everything I knew about the use of mind-altering substances.

Eventually he completed his search and closed my luggage. One thing was perfectly obvious at the end of our encounter: We both felt very good about it.

A more quixotic self stands revealed. I'm not sure that I would have precisely the same conversation today. I would not lie, but I probably wouldn't work quite so hard to open such a novel channel of communication. Nevertheless, I still find that a willingness to be honest—especially about things that one might be expected to conceal—often leads to much more gratifying exchanges with other human beings.

Of course, if I had been carrying illegal drugs, my situation would have been very different. One of the worst things about breaking the law is that it puts you at odds with an indeterminate number of other people. This is among the many corrosive effects of unjust laws: They tempt peaceful and (otherwise) honest people to lie so as to avoid being punished for behavior that is ethically blameless.

Mental Accounting

One of the greatest problems for the liar is that he must keep track of his lies. Some people are better at this than others. Psychopaths can assume the burden of mental accounting without any obvious distress. That is no accident: They are *psychopaths*. They do not care about others and are quite happy to sever relationships whenever the need arises. Some people are monsters of egocentricity. But lying unquestionably comes at a psychological cost for the rest of us.

Lies beget other lies. Unlike statements of fact, which require no further work on our part, lies must be continually protected from collisions with reality. When you tell the truth, you have nothing to keep track of. The world itself becomes your memory, and if questions arise, you can always point others back to it. You can even reconsider certain facts and honestly change your views. And you can openly discuss your confusion, conflicts, and doubts with all comers. A commitment to the truth is naturally purifying of error.

But the liar must remember what he said, and to whom, and must take care to maintain his falsehoods in the future. This can require an extraordinary amount of work—all of which comes at the expense of authentic communication and free attention. The liar must weigh each new disclosure, whatever the source, to see whether it might damage the facade he has built. And all these stresses accrue, whether or not anyone discovers that he has been lying.

Tell enough lies, and the effort needed to keep your audience in the dark eventually becomes unsustainable. While you might be spared a direct accusation of dishonesty, many people will conclude, for reasons they might be unable to pinpoint, that they cannot trust you. You will begin to seem like someone who is always dancing around the facts—because you most certainly are. Many of us have known people like this. No one ever quite confronts them, but everyone begins to treat them like creatures of fiction. Such people are often quietly shunned, for reasons they probably never understand.

In fact, suspicion often grows on *both* sides of a lie: Research indicates that liars trust those they deceive less than they otherwise might—and the more damaging their lies, the less they trust, or even like, their victims. It seems that in protecting their egos and interpreting their own behavior as justified, liars tend to deprecate the people they lie to.[13]

Integrity

What does it mean to have integrity? Integrity consists of many things, but it generally requires us to avoid behavior that readily leads to shame or remorse. The ethical terrain here extends well beyond the question of honesty—but to truly have integrity, we must not feel the need to lie about our personal lives.

To lie is to erect a boundary between the truth we are living and the perception others have of us. The temptation to do this is often born of an understanding that others will disapprove of our behavior. Often, they would have good reason to do so.

Pick up any newspaper and look at the problems people create for themselves—and then attempt to conceal—by lying. It is simply astonishing how people destroy their marriages, careers, and reputations by saying one thing and doing another. Lance Armstrong, Tiger Woods, John Edwards, Eliot Spitzer, Anthony

Wiener—these are men whose names conjure images of the most public self-destruction. Of course, their transgressions weren't merely a matter of lying. But deception was what prepared the ground for their humiliation. One can get divorced without having to issue a public apology. One can even use illegal drugs or live a life of sexual promiscuity or exhibitionism without paying the penalties these men paid. Many lives are almost scandal-proof. Vulnerability comes in pretending to be someone you are not.

Big Lies

Most of us are now painfully aware that our trust in government, corporations, and other public institutions has been undermined by lies.

Lying has prolonged or precipitated wars: The Gulf of Tonkin incident in Vietnam and false reports of weapons of mass destruction in Iraq were both instances in which lying (at some level) led to armed conflict that might otherwise not have occurred. When the truth finally emerged, vast numbers of people grew more cynical about U.S. foreign policy—and many have come to doubt the legitimacy of any military intervention, whatever the stated motive.

Pharmaceutical companies have been widely criticized for misleading the public about the safety and efficacy of their drugs. This misinformation comes in many degrees, but some of it is surely the result of conscious attempts to rig the data. New drugs are often compared with placebos rather than with standard therapies—and when they are compared with an existing drug, it is often given in the wrong dosage. More egregious still, pharmaceutical companies routinely throw out negative results. The epidemiologist Ben Goldacre reports that for certain drugs more than 50 percent of the trial data has been withheld. Consequently, industry-funded trials are four times as likely to show the benefits of a new drug.[14]

Big lies have led many people to reflexively distrust those in positions of authority. As a result, it is now impossible to say anything of substance on climate change, environmental pollution, human nutrition, economic policy, foreign conflicts, medicine, and dozens of other subjects without a significant percentage of one's audience expressing paralyzing doubts about even the most reputable sources of information. Our public discourse appears permanently riven by conspiracy theories.[15]

Consider the widespread fear of childhood vaccinations. In 1998, the physician Andrew Wakefield published a study in *The Lancet* linking the measles, mumps, and rubella (MMR) vaccine to autism. This study has since been judged to be an "elaborate fraud," and Wakefield's medical license has been revoked.[16]

The consequences of Wakefield's dishonesty would have been bad enough. But the legacy effect of other big lies has thus far made it impossible to remedy the damage he caused. Given the fact that corporations and governments sometimes lie, whether to avoid legal liability or to avert public panic, it has become very difficult to spread the truth about the MMR vaccine. Vaccination rates have plummeted—especially in prosperous, well-educated communities—and children have become sick and even died as a result.

An unhappy fact about human psychology is probably at work here, which makes it hard to abolish lies once they have escaped into the world: We seem to be predisposed to remember statements as true even after they have been disconfirmed. For instance, if a rumor spreads that a famous politician once fainted during a campaign speech, and the story is later revealed to be false, some significant percentage of people will recall it as true—even if they were first exposed to it in the very context of its debunking. In psychology, this is known as the "illusory truth effect." Familiarity breeds credence.

One can imagine circumstances, perhaps in time of war, in which lying to one's enemies might be necessary—especially if spreading misinformation was likely to reduce the loss of innocent life. Granted, the boundary between these conditions and many of the cases cited above might be difficult to spot—especially if lying to one's enemies entails also lying to one's friends. In such circumstances, we might recognize a good lie only in retrospect. But war and espionage are conditions in which human relationships have broken down or were never established in the first place; thus the usual rules of cooperation no longer apply. The moment one begins dropping bombs, or destroying a country's infrastructure with cyber attacks, lying has become just another weapon in the arsenal.

The need for state secrets is obvious. However, the need for governments to lie to their own people seems to me to be virtually nonexistent. Justified government deception is a kind of ethical mirage: Just when you think you're reaching it, the facts usually suggest otherwise. And the harm occasioned whenever lies of this kind are uncovered is all but irreparable.

I suspect that the telling of necessary lies will be rare for anyone but a spy—assuming we grant that espionage is ethically defensible in today's world. It is rumored that spies must lie even to their friends and family. I am quite sure that I could not live this way myself, however good the cause. The role of a spy strikes me as a near total sacrifice of personal ethics for a larger good—whether real or imagined. It is a kind of moral self-immolation.

But I think we can draw no more daily instruction from the lives of spies than we can from the adventures of astronauts in space. Just as most of us need not worry about our bone density in the absence of gravity, we need not consider whether our every utterance could compromise national security. The ethics of war and espionage are the ethics of emergency—and are, therefore, necessarily limited in scope.

Conclusion

As it was in *Anna Karenina*, *Madame Bovary*, and *Othello*, so it is in life. Most forms of private vice and public evil are kindled and sustained by lies. Acts of adultery and other personal betrayals, financial fraud, government corruption—even murder and genocide—generally require an additional moral defect: a willingness to lie.

Lying is, almost by definition, a refusal to cooperate with others. It condenses a lack of trust and trustworthiness into a single act. It is both a failure of understanding and an unwillingness to be understood. To lie is to recoil from relationship.

By lying, we deny others our view of the world. And our dishonesty not only influences the choices they make, it often determines the choices they *can* make—in ways we cannot always predict. Every lie is an assault on the autonomy of those we lie to.

By lying to one person, we potentially spread falsehoods to many others—even to whole societies. We also force upon ourselves subsequent choices—to maintain the deception or not—that can complicate our lives. In this way, every lie haunts our future. We can't tell when or how it might collide with reality, requiring further maintenance. The truth never needs to be tended like this. It can simply be reiterated.

The lies of the powerful lead us to distrust governments and corporations. The lies of the weak make us callous toward the suffering of others. The lies of conspiracy theorists raise doubts about the honesty of whistle-blowers, even when they are telling the truth.[17] Lies are the social equivalent of toxic waste: Everyone is potentially harmed by their spread.

How would your relationships change if you resolved never to lie again? What truths about yourself might suddenly come into view? What kind of person would you become? And how might you change the people around you?

It is worth finding out.

A Conversation with Ronald A. Howard

As I wrote in the introduction, Ronald A. Howard was one of my favorite professors in college, and his courses on ethics, social systems, and decision making did much to shape my views on these topics. Howard directs teaching and research in the Decision Analysis Program of the Department of Management Science and Engineering at Stanford University. He is also the director of the department's Decisions and Ethics Center, which examines the efficacy and ethics of social arrangements. He defined the profession of decision analysis in 1964 and has since supervised several doctoral theses on decision analysis every year. His experience includes dozens of decision analysis projects that range over virtually all fields of application, from investment planning to research strategy, and from hurricane seeding to nuclear waste isolation. He was a founding director and chairman of Strategic Decisions Group and is the president of the Decision Education Foundation, an organization dedicated to bringing decision skills to youth. He is a member of the National Academy of Engineering, a fellow of INFORMS and IEEE, and the 1986 Ramsey medalist of the Decision Analysis Society. He is also the author, with Clint Korver, of *Ethics for the Real World*.

For the hardcover edition of this book, he was kind enough to speak with me about the ethics of lying. The following is an edited transcript of our conversation.

. . .

Harris: First, let me say that I greatly appreciate your taking the time to do this interview. As you may or may not know, your courses on ethics at Stanford were pivotal in my moral and intellectual development—as they have surely been for many others. So it's an honor to be able to bring your voice to my readers.

Howard: My pleasure.

Harris: Let's talk about lying. I think we might as well start with the hardest case for the truth-teller: The Nazis are at the door, and you've got Anne Frank hiding in the attic. How do you think about situations in which honesty seems to open the door—in this case literally—to moral catastrophe?

Howard: As you point out, these are very difficult situations to think through, and one hopes that one would be able to transform them. In other words, if you were the Buddha or some other remarkable person, perhaps some version of the truth could still save the day. You probably remember the story of the Buddha's encountering a murderer who had killed 1,000 people. Instead of avoiding him, he said, "I know you're going to kill me, but would you first cut off the large branch on that tree?" The murderer does so, and then the Buddha says, "Thank you. Now would you put it back on?" And—the story goes—the murderer suddenly realized that he was playing the wrong game in life, and became enlightened and a monk.

It's not inconceivable that one could transform even a terribly dire situation—and I think that doing so would constitute a kind of moral perfection. Of course, that's pretty hard to imagine for most of us when confronted by Nazis at the door. But there are extreme cases in which, depending on the participants, it's not clear that telling the truth will always lead to a bad outcome.

Harris: I agree. But it's probably setting the bar too high for most of us, most of the time—and, more important, it is surely setting it too high for any randomly selected group of Nazis. It seems that there are situations in which one must admit at the outset that one is not in the presence of an ethical intelligence that can be reasoned with.

I take your point, however, that if one makes that determination—these are not Nazis I'm going to be able to enlighten—one has closed the door to certain kinds of moral breakthrough. For instance, I remember hearing about a rabbi who was receiving threatening calls from a white supremacist. Rather than hang up or call the police, the rabbi patiently heard the man out, every time he called, whatever the hour. Eventually they started having a real conversation, and ultimately the rabbi broke through, and the white supremacist started telling him about all the troubles in his life. They even met and became friends. One certainly likes to believe that such breakthroughs are possible.

Nevertheless, in some situations the threat is so obvious, and the time in which one must make a judgment so brief, that one must err on the side of treating an avowed enemy as a real enemy.

Howard: Of course. And some people deal with this by thinking in a kind of a hierarchy. They might say, "Well,

I don't want to kill people, but I'll kill in self-defense. I don't want to steal, but I'd steal to keep someone alive. I wouldn't ordinarily lie, but I'll do it to save someone's property or to save a life, and so forth. That's another way to handle it.

Harris: That is the way I handled it in my book. Essentially, I view lying in these cases as an extension of the continuum of force one would use against a person who appears no longer capable of a rational conversation. If you would be willing to defensively shoot a person who had come to harm you or someone in your care, or you would be willing to punch him in the jaw, it seems ethical to use even less force—that is, mere speech—to deflect his bad intentions.

Howard: I think that's a very practical solution. We are beginning to speak here about the part of one's ethical code that one is willing to impose on other people, which I refer to by the maxim "Peaceful, honest people have the right to be left alone." It simplifies things to ask, "What if someone violates this maxim by not behaving in ways that I would like people to behave—leaving innocent people alone, and so forth?" Then I reserve the right of self-defense. If someone is trying to kill me, I'm going to use the minimum effective force necessary to stop him. I read your article[18] on this, and I agree with you completely.

The next level is stealing: Needless to say, if I could steal a weapon from someone who was about to kill me, that would be fine. And if I couldn't transform the situation as some more enlightened person might—into a real circumstance of teaching—then I would lie. I would use the minimum distortion necessary to get the problem to go away.

At one end of the spectrum, you can be super-optimistic about people. But let's face it, there are people who are up to no good in all kinds of ways. I'm not going to abet them in violating other people's right to be left alone, and I'll do whatever is necessary to avoid that.

Harris: Obviously, the Anne Frank case doesn't often arise in the ordinary course of life, but there are many other troubling situations in which people find it tempting to lie. When I asked for feedback from readers on the first edition of *Lying*, I received many accounts in which people found themselves lying for reasons that they thought entirely noble. One case I'd like you to reflect on relates to a terminally ill child.

Your child doesn't have long to live. Naturally, he has questions about when he will die and about what happens after death. Let's say that given what the doctor has said, you think your child has about two months to live. You also believe that everyone gets a dial tone after death and that you'll never see each other again. Many readers find it hard to avoid the conclusion that giving a false but consoling response to his questions could make your child's last two months of life happier than they would otherwise be.

Howard: Well, that's a case where I would take a much stronger position. I've had people in my classes who regularly deal with the dying, and their advice is always the same: You should tell the truth as you believe it to be. The important thing to determine is, what is the truth? So you ask the doctor, "Doctor, how long has he got?" and the truthful answer might be "Well, you know, some people surprise us, some people go quicker. We really can't tell you exactly how long. Most people have two months, but a few live longer, and so on." Now, that's the truth. If you said, "Oh, no, you're going to recover," when he's probably going to die in a few months, you would deprive the person of the opportunity to do all those things that he or she might want to do in this limited time. In most cases, they know they're dying. Let them go peacefully.

Once, a man in a group meeting shared that his young son was terminally ill. He said, "You know, it's really sad: When he colors pictures, he uses only the black crayons." Then, after one week, he spoke to the group again. He said, "You know what? I realized that I was holding myself back from my son because I was going to miss him so much after he dies." He shared that truth with his son, telling him, "I love you so much, and I'm going to miss you." And guess what? He reported that the boy was now using all the colors.

My understanding from people who deal with kids who are dying is that they know. The parents are really grieving for all the experiences that they're not going to have with their child. The child isn't thinking, "I'm not going to get married." That's not in his knowing at that point, unless you dump it on him. He may not see his dog again, but that's not the same thing as the parents' grief over all that they're anticipating losing over a lifetime.

Harris: So, the truth that exists to be told to the child is not the same as the parents' anticipated loss, or their ideas about what the child himself will be losing.

Howard: Right. Telling the kid "It's really sad you're dying because you're not going to get married" misses the point. You might as well say, "You're also not going to serve in the army. You're not going to kill people.

You're not going to experience the death of other people that you love." You see? That's life. It doesn't all have a Hollywood ending. There are lots of pluses and minuses. Ultimately, we all die, and the only question is, what have you done between the time you're born and the time you die? Did you make the most of this unique opportunity?

Harris: I agree with all that. But cases of this kind suggest certain caveats to scrupulous truth-telling. There still seems to be a tension between honesty and our responsibility to protect children and other people whom we might judge to be less than competent to deal with the truth as we see it. So, let's say you take all the time required to figure out what the truth really is, and yet you are in the presence of someone, whether a child or an adult, who you think needs to be spared certain truths. Other examples of this have come to me from people who are caring for parents with dementia. Your mother wakes up every morning wondering where your father is, but your father has been dead for fifteen years. Every time you explain this, your mother has to relive the bereavement process all over again, only to wake up the next morning looking for her husband. Let's assume that when you lie, saying something like "Oh, he's away on a business trip," your mother very quickly forgets about your father's absence and her grief doesn't get reactivated.

Howard: That's an interesting one. I would be tempted to say something more like "Well, he's where he usually is at this time of day." The fact that he's buried in the ground somewhere doesn't add anything to this person's knowledge of what's going on. As you point out, you would just be putting her through pain all over again. As you stated the case, why would you want to do that?

Harris: What you seem to be acknowledging here, however, is that it is okay to be somewhat evasive in situations of this kind. At the very least, it can take some skill to thread the needle and find a truth that is appropriate to the other person's situation.

Howard: I'd call it "skillful truth-telling" as opposed to "evasion," in the sense that if this person could look at the whole conversation—let's say she magically gets better again and can say, "Oh, I had Alzheimer's. How did you deal with me when I kept asking about Dad?"—she would look at the transcript and say, "You know, that's right. In my mind, he was someplace, and I just didn't know where he was. What you said allowed me to get out of that loop." That's fine.

Harris: I'm just going to keep throwing difficult cases at you, Ron.

Howard: You go right ahead.

Harris: Let's again invoke a deathbed scene, where the dying person asks, "Did you ever cheat in our marriage?" Let's say it's a wife asking her husband. The truthful answer is that he did cheat on her. However, the truth of their relationship—*now*—is that this is completely irrelevant. And yet it is also true that he took great pains to conceal the betrayal from her at one point, and he has kept quiet about it ever since. What good could come from telling the truth in that situation?

Howard: Well, this is really a two-part problem, and the first part is, why would this husband want to live a lie all his life?

Harris: I agree. But we have to put a frame around the relevant facts of the present, and if a person hasn't been perfectly ethical up until yesterday, he has to figure out how to live with the legacy of his misbehavior. This thing is buried in the past. He hasn't thought about it in forever, but the truth is that he did cheat on his wife, and now she's asking about it. In his mind, he seems to have a choice between lying and having a perfectly loving last few days or weeks of his marriage, and breaking his wife's heart for no good reason.

Howard: Well, this is one of those textbook situations that we sometimes get into in ethics class. The terrorists get aboard the plane and try to make you kill a little old lady, threatening that they're going to shoot everybody else if you don't. Life doesn't really work like that. I know of very few marriages, for example, where the husband has cheated and the wife didn't suspect it.

Harris: I can't let you off that easily. I think there's something realistic about a case like this. We can even grant that she did suspect it all those years, and she buried her suspicion. Now she's on her deathbed and she finally wants the truth, for whatever reason.

Howard: Then they've had a silent conspiracy to not talk about this thing their whole life. Now what? In other words, she bears the responsibility as much as he does. The question is, are they going to start living an open life now and be truthful to each other, or not? They could do it. He could say, "We've never talked about this. Is this something you really want to talk about today?" This may be the time, whatever their beliefs about what happens after death. Or he could say, "Look, we've got a very short time together, and whatever we've done in the past, if it doesn't bring us joy now, let's leave it behind."

Harris: It's interesting—there seems to be an odd intuition working in cases like this, which I only just noticed in myself: If we shorten the time horizon to a few days, or a few weeks, or even a few months, it can appear to undermine the rationale for living truthfully. Many people seem to feel that if we have only two weeks left together, it's probably better to live a consoling lie, but if we have 20 years left, then we might want to put our house in order and live truthfully.

Howard: I look at it another way: No matter how much time I've got left, I want to live a life that I have no regrets about.

Harris: I agree. But I think a moral illusion may be creeping in here. When you dial the remainder of someone's life down to a very short span, people begin to wonder, what good could possibly come from telling the truth? In my view, one might as well apply that thinking to the whole of life.

Howard: Absolutely. This gets to the very foundation of what we're talking about here, which is how you want to live your life and care for the people in it. My father used to talk about someone's being a man of his word, and I guess maybe it's sexist these days, but I never hear that anymore. Clint Korver, the doctoral student who has helped me teach my course and write our ethics book, was once introduced at a conference, quite correctly, as "the guy who always tells the truth." I find it absolutely shocking that anyone would need to mention that. It's like saying he doesn't steal or murder people. Why not say, "And he breathes, too"? "He's lived for many years, and he's been breathing all this time." Great. Glad to hear it.

Harris: It just indicates how commonplace lying is. It's ubiquitous, and most people don't even consider what life would be like without it.

Another difficult case comes to mind, also from a reader: You're having sex with your wife or husband and fantasizing about someone else. Later, your spouse has the temerity to ask what you were thinking about when you were having sex. The honest answer is that you were thinking about someone else. But let's say that you know your spouse will not do well with this information. He or she will view it as a real breach of trust, rather than just a natural consequence of having a human imagination.

Howard: Well, that's another case in which, when you first suspect this, it's probably time to have a conversation. Just what is okay? Is it "whatever turns you on"?—you know, "I could be the pirate and you could be the helpless maiden . . ." and so forth. Is that okay? Or is it "Oh, my god, you're not seeing me as I really am." People will obviously differ in this area, but couples need to have an honest conversation about it. I think honesty really is all that matters. It transforms the situation.

Why would you want to live a lie in your sex life? It seems silly to live a life of pretense, and it's okay to have fantasies. Why not say, "Look, if it turns you on to think that I'm Brad Pitt, it's going to be more fun for me when you're turned on, so go for it. Because that's why I'm here in the first place, right? I love you, and I want to have the best life with you that we can have."

Harris: I can feel our readers abandoning us in droves, but I agree with you. Let's return to a case in which you are in the presence of someone who seems likely to act unethically. Can you say more about honesty in those situations?

Howard: Well, I'd make a distinction between the maxim-breakers—in other words, people who are harming others or stealing—and those who are merely lying or otherwise speaking unethically. Lying is not a crime unless it's part of a fraud. If someone asks for directions to Walmart, and you know the way but you send him walking in the opposite direction—it's not a nice thing to do, but it's not a crime. Imagine if he came back with a policeman and said, "That's the man who misdirected me." You could say, "Yeah, I did. It just so happens that I like to watch people wandering in the wrong direction." That's not a crime.[19] It's not nice behavior. It might be reason for someone to boycott your business, or to exclude you from certain groups, but it's not going to land you in jail.

I make a careful distinction between what I call "maxim violations"—interfering with peaceful, honest people—and everything else.

Harris: Yes, I see. It breaks ethics into two categories—one of which gets promoted to the legal system to protect people from various harms.

Howard: In fact, there are also two categories in the domain of lying. The first is where people acknowledge the problem—people obviously get hurt by lies—and the other is cases where more or less everyone tends to lie and feels good about it, or sees no alternative to it. That's why your book is so important—because people think it's a good thing to tell so-called "white" lies. Saying "Oh, you look terrific in that dress" even when you believe it is unattractive is a white lie justified by not hurting the person's feelings.

The example that came up in class yesterday was, do you want that mirror-mirror-on-the-wall-who's-the-fairest-of-them-all device, or do you want a mirror that shows you what you really look like? Or imagine buying a car that came with a special option that gave you information you might prefer to the truth: When you wanted to go fast, it would indicate that you were going even faster than you were. When you passed a gas station, it would tell you that you didn't need any gas. Of course, nobody wants that. Well, then, why would you want it in your life in general?

Harris: However, there are some arguments, from both an evolutionary and a psychological perspective, that suggest that having one's beliefs ever so slightly out of register with reality can be adaptive and psychologically helpful. I'm sure you're familiar with the research that shows that if he's brought into a room full of strangers to give a brief speech, a depressed person will tend to accurately judge what sort of impression he has made, while a normal person will tend to overestimate how positively others saw him. It's hard to know which is cause and which is effect here—but it does seem that optimism bias could be psychologically advantageous.

Howard: It might have allowed people to survive a lot better in the past.

Harris: Yes. In fact, self-deception might have paid evolutionary dividends in other ways. Robert Trivers argues, for instance, that people who can believe their own lies turn out to be the best liars of all—and an ability to deceive rivals has obvious advantages in the state of nature. Now, clearly many things may have been adaptive for our ancestors—such as tribal warfare, rape, xenophobia—that we now deem unethical and would never want to defend. But I'm wondering if you see any possibility that a social system that maximizes truth-telling could be one that fails to maximize the well-being of all participants. Is it possible that some measure of deception is good for us?

Howard: This gets back to distinctions I make between prudential, ethical, and legal principles. Is the statement "Honesty is the best policy" a prudential statement? In other words, is it merely in your interest to be honest? That's different from saying, "I am ethically committed to being honest," because you could probably find individual circumstances where dishonesty gives you an advantage.

I think that growth is encouraged by accurate feedback. Telling children they are always accomplishing wonderful things regardless of their actual accomplishments is not going to serve them when they face the world. Having a positive mental attitude toward life is prudential, but being overconfident in your abilities is not.

A student yesterday said that he had recently bid for something, and he told the guy that he didn't have enough money to pay the full price. But that was a lie. He really had the money, but he said, "I only have X," and the seller said, "Okay. I'll give it to you for X, if that's all the money you have." So my student was feeling pretty good about this negotiation because from his point of view, he saved money by telling an untruth. But the seller could have said, "Sorry. I've got other offers at the price X+1," in which case my student would have been exposed in his lie if he really wanted the item and said, "Okay, I'll pay X+1 too." This all gets to the question of whether you have repeated relationships. Do you view your life in terms of relationships or transactions?

If you're bidding on eBay, truth isn't an issue. That is a completely transactional situation. If I'm dealing with my mechanic on an ongoing basis, it's not a transaction. It's a relationship, and he will make judgments about me and about my reliability as a person. And I will make judgments about him, and these judgments will have long-term effects for both of us. This alters the prisoner's dilemma: If you have a relationship with a person, you're going to have different beliefs about the prospect of his selling you out than you would if he were just some guy the experimenters grabbed and put in the situation with you.

I don't think you can get from "is" to "ought" in the coarse sense of saying that ethical people make more money, are always happier, and so forth. That would be to prove that it is always prudential to be ethical. Now, I personally believe it generally is, but I can't prove that.

Harris: I agree. But you seem to have a very strong intuition, which I share, that we should consider honesty to be a nearly ironclad principle, because it is to everyone's advantage so much of the time, and it allows us to live the kinds of lives and maintain the kinds of relationships we want to have.

Howard: I believe it also extends to truths about oneself. Self-deception isn't of any value either. For instance, I was never going to be a professional singer. If I didn't understand this fact about myself, people could have said, "Oh, you're a great singer. You ought to quit your job and start recording." But that's just bullshit. You've got to be honest about who you are—about what you know and don't know and about what you can and can't do—and still be willing to try things and experiment. To me, it's pretty simple.

Harris: And, needless to say, it makes sense to want to be in touch with reality. Given that your every move in life will be constrained by whatever the facts are, both out in the world and in the minds of others, being guided by anything less than these facts will leave you perpetually vulnerable to embarrassment and disappointment. When your model of yourself in the world is at odds with how you actually are in the world, you are going to keep bumping into things.

I think where people get confused, psychologically and ethically, is when they consider that part of reality that exists only in the minds of others. The question is, do you really want to know what other people think about you—about your talents and prospects—or do you want to be deceived about all that?

Many people imagine that they want to be protected from the knowledge of what other people really think, because they believe their own performance in the world will be best served by this ignorance. I think they're mistaken, but it's interesting to consider cases where they might be right.

Howard: It is—and that gets down to the question of what your view is toward life as a whole. I tend to go back to something like the Buddha's eightfold path. I remember once hearing a Buddhist speaker give a talk, and at question time a woman said, "I was raised as a Christian, where the idea of charity is built in, and yet you haven't mentioned charity at all. So I'm having trouble understanding your ethics."

And he said to her, "Well, when you were doing all these charitable things"—which she said she regularly did at church, helping people all over the world, sending them baskets and stuff—"did you really care about the people you were doing these things for?" The woman was silent for a moment and then she said, "No. I hadn't really thought about that." And the teacher said, "Well, when you care, you'll know what to do."

That's so different from saying, "You've got to be charitable." When you actually care about the experience of other people, you tend to know what to do. The conversation you and I are having now is kind of like writing a manual for unenlightened people like ourselves, so we won't all make too many mistakes along the way.

I sometimes use a metaphor of the guy who never knew he had to put oil in his new car, because no one ever told him. He never read the manual, and now after three years the engine is burned out. He takes the car into the shop, and the mechanic says, "Hey, you have to put oil in these things. Now your engine is ruined." And the man says, "Oh, if only I'd known!" You see, he had no intention of creating this problem that he now has to solve. Well, in speaking about ethics, you and I are trying to raise everyone's sensibilities so that we can all live in a preemptive way, as opposed to saying, "Oh my god, what was I thinking?" later on.

Harris: That's what I felt when I first took your course at Stanford. It was as if I had been given part of the user's manual to a good life, and by following the simple principle of telling the truth, I could bypass most of the needless misery I read about in literature and witnessed in the lives of other people. I remember leaving your course feeling that I had discovered a bomb at the very center of my life and had been given the tools to defuse it before it could do any damage. It was a tremendous relief.

I've begun to wonder, however, at what level the ethical problems we see in the world can best be addressed. The level we tend to speak about, as we have here, is that of a person's personal ethical code and his individual approach to life, moment to moment. But I suspect that the biggest returns come at the level of changing social norms and institutions—that is, in creating systems that align people's priorities so that it becomes much easier for ordinary people to behave more ethically than they do when they are surrounded by perverse incentives. For instance, a person usually has to be a hero to be a whistle-blower, given that he will most likely lose his job for telling the truth. But in a culture of honesty, it becomes much easier to be truthful. I'm interested in those changes we can make that will cause all boats to rise with the same tide.

Howard: Right. And in my own life I know that I don't want to do business with people that I'm not on the same ethical wavelength with, so to speak. No matter how attractive the deal looks, if I don't trust these people—in the sense that you and I are talking about—I don't want to do business with them, no matter how profitable it might be.

But the problem is that a lot of our life today is transactional. I just bought something from Amazon.com, and there was nobody there, so to speak. It was just credit cards and button clicks. If you go to the supermarket today, the laser system tells you what the price is and the checker bags it for you. In the old days it might be, "Oh, you bought a lot of spaghetti. Do you have sauce for that?" There's no feeling that the checker is a partner in this experience of buying something.

I have this example of what I call the "hardware store hammer": A woman is in a hardware store and picks up a hammer. When she is checking out, the shop owner says, "What are you going to use this hammer for?" And she says, "My husband told me to buy a hammer. We're putting up some pictures in the kitchen." The owner might say, "Okay. But this is a professional carpenter's hammer. For your purpose, that one over there would do just fine, and it's a third the price." That's the difference between a relationship and a transaction. If you have a concern that other people do well for themselves, then I think you want this level of honesty. But our society might be losing that.

We have a great technological advantage, but it's not like when my father ran a grocery store. If the kids didn't arrive with enough money, he knew who was who, and it was not a problem. They could just bring the money next time. You don't see much of that today. Now you've got your credit card, and the idea of extending that kind of trust and courtesy just doesn't come up anymore. So certain kinds of relationships seem less possible.

Harris: Yes, a system-wide change can either facilitate our ethical connections to other people or erode them. This brings me to a related question: Are there some things that are important to do—that is, ultimately ethical to do—but which require that the person doing them sacrifice his ethics? I bring this up briefly in the book when I talk about spying. The position I take is that there are certain jobs I know I would not want to do, and I suspect that they are intrinsically toxic for the person who has to do them, but I can't say I think those jobs are unnecessary. I'm thinking of things such as espionage and research on animals. I know I don't want to be the guy who saws the scalps off rats all day, but I'd be hard-pressed to say we shouldn't be using rats in medical research. So, assuming you are going to grant that espionage is occasionally necessary, what do you think about the lifetime of lying entailed by working at the CIA?

Howard: You could also consider what it's like to be an undercover police officer.

Harris: Yes, that might be an even simpler case— assuming the laws he is working to enforce are good ones. I know you and I agree on how harmful the war on drugs has been. If an undercover cop were deceiving people to enforce drug laws, I think we would both question the ethics of that line of work.

Howard: Exactly. I'd want to first make sure the cop is enforcing good laws. If it's a serial rapist found, that's fine. I'm happy to have police who are out there finding those people and bringing them to justice. We all pay a huge price for living in a world with people who are maxim-breakers. I wish we could live in a world where no one had to use passwords, for instance. But we have passwords and burglar alarms and keys . . . If you go out in the country, people say, "You mean you don't leave your key in the car? And you lock your house?"

That's why I want a very strong system to deter maxim-breakers based on restitution. In other words, some of these things you do are imposing costs on everyone else. I've never been burglarized, but I'm paying the price for people who commit burglary, through insurance and other costs. If you engage in that sort of behavior, you ought to pay the overhead for it. But that's a longer story.

Harris: I agree on this point as well. Insofar as it is possible, our justice system should oblige criminals to repay their debts to society rather than pointlessly suffer on account of them.

Howard: The trouble is, we can't separate these things when we get into the kind of discussion we're having now: What kind of crimes are there in society, and how do you find the people who are perpetrating them? What kind of judgment do they get, and what are the penalties for having done these things? This is a book all in itself, but it's extremely important.

Harris: No doubt. Well, Ron, this has been great, and I think readers will find your thoughts on all these topics very useful. Thank you for taking the time to speak with me. And let me say again, in case I never told you personally, that the courses you taught at Stanford were probably the most important I ever took. It's rare that one sees wisdom being directly imparted in an academic setting. But that is what you did, and have continued to do for decades. So I just want to say, "Thank you."

Howard: You are very welcome. And it was great to have this conversation.

A Conversation with Readers

The following questions and comments came from readers of the original e-book edition of *Lying*. Most have been edited to emphasize key points.

1. *You seem to suggest that giving false praise or telling "white" lies is akin to treating another person like a child. This leads me to wonder whether you think it's morally acceptable to lie to children.*

As parents, we must maintain our children's trust—and it seems to me that the easiest way to lose it is by lying to them. Of course, we should communicate the truth in ways that they can handle—and this often demands that we suppress details that would be confusing or needlessly disturbing. An important difference between children and (normal) adults is that children are not fully capable of conceiving of (much less looking out for) their real interests. Consequently, it might be necessary in some situations to pacify or motivate them with a lie. In my experience, however, such circumstances almost never arise. My daughter is nearly five, and I can recall lying to her only once. We were looking for nursery rhymes on the Internet and landed on a page that showed a 16th-century woodcut of a person being decapitated. As I was hurriedly scrolling elsewhere, she demanded to know what we had just seen. I said something silly like "That was an old and very impractical form of surgery." This left her suitably perplexed, and she remains unaware of man's inhumanity to man to this day. However, I doubt that even this lie was necessary. I just wasn't thinking very fast on my feet.

The problem of false praise also rarely arises with children. Especially with young children, the purpose of praise is to encourage them to try new things and enjoy themselves in the process. It isn't a matter of evaluating their performance by reference to some external standard. The truth communicated by saying "That's amazing" or "I love it" in response to a child's drawing is never difficult to find or feel. Things change when one is talking to an adult who wants to know how his work compares with the work of others.

2. What should we tell our children about Santa? My daughter asked if Santa was real the other day, and I couldn't bear to disappoint her.

Strangely, this is the most common question I've received from readers. In fact, I heard from several who seemed to expect it would be, and who wrote to tell me how disturbed they had been when they learned that their parents had lied to them every Christmas. I also heard from readers whose parents told the truth about Santa simply because they didn't want the inevitable unraveling of the Christmas myth to cast any doubt on the divinity of Jesus Christ. I suppose some ironies are harder to detect than others.

I don't remember whether I ever believed in Santa, but I was never tempted to tell my daughter that he was real. Christmas must be marginally more exciting for children who are duped about Santa—but something similar could be said of many phenomena about which no one is tempted to lie. Why not insist that dragons, mermaids, fairies, and Superman actually exist? Why not present the work of Tolkien and Rowling as history?

The real truth—which everyone knows 364 days of the year—is that fiction can be both meaningful and fun. Children have fantasy lives so rich and combustible that rigging them with lies is like putting a propeller on a rocket. And is the last child in class who still believes in Santa really grateful to have his first lesson in epistemology meted out by his fellow six-year-olds?

If you deceive your children about Santa, you may give them a more thrilling experience of Christmas. What you probably won't give them, however, is the sense that you would not and could not lie to them about anything else.

3. *The chapter in which you discuss "lies in extremis" contains statements that seem incompatible with the ethical philosophy you advocate in* The Moral Landscape. *The chapter presents a scenario in which a homeowner hides a child from a known murderer and then must choose how to respond when the murderer knocks on the front door demanding information about his quarry's whereabouts. You appear to believe that even in this life-and-death situation, ethical people should privilege strategies that allow them to tell the truth over those that involve lying. In particular, you express a concern "that lying was the easy (and less than perfectly ethical) way out," and suggest that even if the reader thinks it was necessary, that "doesn't mean someone more courageous or capable than you couldn't have produced a better result with the truth."*

Your goals as the homeowner should be to avoid harm to the child, yourself, and other people in the neighborhood while also increasing the chances that the murderer will be apprehended by the police. None of these goals seems well served by provoking the murderer into a potentially violent confrontation at the very house where his target is hiding. The police are an organized, well-trained, and well-armed force that specializes in capturing criminals. Isn't it a needless display of macho bravado to confront the murderer when you know the child is safe inside your house and you can immediately call the police so that they can do what they do best? Even if you felt it was necessary to take matters into your own hands, telling the truth places you at a tactical disadvantage. As you recognize elsewhere in the book, when discussing war and espionage, in violent situations lying is just another weapon that can be used against the enemy.

These are excellent points, and I agree with all of them. However, I think it's important to account for outcomes that are either much better or much worse than those you deem likely in this case. It is at least conceivable that a brave and saintly person could transform the murderer with the truth. As I said in my exchange with Ron Howard, I don't think one can generally recommend this approach, but it seems to me that we must allow that it is possible and grant it a higher spot on the moral landscape than the alternatives. If, for instance, Lao Tzu could invite the man in for tea and get him to repent of his evil and surrender to the police without a fight, that would be the best outcome of all.

Similarly, lying and calling the police might result in a tragedy that could have been prevented by an honest confrontation with evil. The police could take a long time to arrive, and innocent lives could be lost in the interval. There are certainly cases in which decisive action on the part of a brave civilian might have prevented a tremendous amount of human suffering. Again, I'm not saying that most people should be guided by these possibilities, but we must leave space on our ethical map for them.

There is a tension between avoiding danger and resisting evil—and how we resolve it will depend on many factors. If I see a man about to attack another person on the street, should I avoid danger or resist evil? If my five-year-old daughter is with me, I might scoop her up and leave the scene as quickly as possible. If I were a police officer, however, I would have a duty to intervene. In either case it seems perfectly acceptable to lie—because false speech is among the most benign weapons one can use against another human being. One could yell, "The police are coming!" or "Hey! There are cameras all over this block. Do you want to spend years in prison for what you're about to do?" Deception like this might resolve the situation without the need for physical violence. Thus, it makes ethical and tactical sense.

4. *Would you say more about the distinction you made, in your subsequent conversation with Ronald Howard, about the difference between one's personal ethical code and changing social norms/institutions?*

The influence of social systems extends far beyond the problem of lying, and I think changing these norms and institutions represents the greatest hope for improving our ethical lives. Imagine, for instance, that a young, white man has been falsely convicted of a serious crime and sentenced to five years in a maximum-security prison. Let's say this person is highly ethical and has no history of violence. He is, understandably, terrified at the prospect of living among murderers and rapists. When he hears the prison gates shut behind him, a lifetime of diverse interests and aspirations will collapse to a single point: He must avoid making enemies so that he can serve out his sentence in peace.

Unfortunately, our hero is about to encounter the limited utility of having a personal ethical code. Prisons are places of perverse incentives, in which the very norms one must follow to avoid becoming a victim lead inescapably toward violence. In most U.S. prisons, for instance, whites, blacks, and Hispanics exist in a state of perpetual war. This young man is not a racist, and he would prefer to interact peacefully with everyone he meets, but if he does not join a gang, he is likely to be targeted for rape and other abuse by prisoners of all races. To not choose a side is to become the most attractive victim of all. Being white, he most likely will have no rational option but to join a white-supremacist gang for protection.

So he joins a gang. In order to remain a member in good standing, however, he must be willing to defend other gang members, no matter how sociopathic their behavior. He also discovers that he must be prepared to use violence at the tiniest provocation—returning a verbal insult with a stabbing, for instance—or risk acquiring a reputation as someone who can be assaulted at will. To fail to respond with overwhelming force to the first sign of disrespect is to run an intolerable risk of further abuse. Thus, the young man begins behaving in precisely those ways that make every maximum-security prison a hell on earth. He also adds further time to his sentence by committing serious crimes behind bars.

A prison is perhaps the easiest place to see the power of bad incentives. And yet in many walks of life, we find otherwise normal men and women caught in the same trap and busily making the world much less good than it could be. Elected officials ignore long-term problems because they must pander to the short-term interests of voters. People working for insurance companies rely on technicalities to deny desperately ill patients the care they need. CEOs and investment bankers run extraordinary risks—both for their businesses and for the economy as a whole—because they reap the rewards of success without suffering the penalties of failure. District attorneys continue to prosecute people they know to be innocent because their careers depend on winning cases. Our government fights a war on drugs that creates the very problem of black-market profits and violence that it pretends to solve.

We need systems that are wiser than we are. We need institutions and cultural norms that make us more honest and ethical than we tend to be. The project of building them is distinct from—and, in my view, even more important than—an individual's refining his personal ethical code.

5. *I'm a journalist, so I often think about Janet Malcolm's classic text when I'm doing an interview. Should I be honest with my subject and say straight out that I am using him to tell a story that he may not be happy to have made public? The answer is not clear. What if Truman Capote had been honest with the people he interviewed for* In Cold Blood? *Would we be better off without that book? Or would we be better off with a book in which the subjects were more fully informed? The trouble is, they might have refused to participate.*

This strikes me as a genuinely difficult question of journalistic ethics. As Malcolm observed, strange bonds of trust and self-deception tend to grow between journalists and their subjects. She examined these fraught encounters in a fascinating book, *The Journalist and the Murderer*, which focused on the relationship between Joe McGinniss, the best-selling author of *Fatal Vision*, and Jeffrey MacDonald, a Green Beret physician convicted of murdering his pregnant wife and two young daughters.

Malcolm's book is especially interesting for its diagnosis of the ethical problems surrounding the standard print interview:

> Every journalist who is not too stupid or too full
> of himself to notice what is going on knows that what

he does is morally indefensible. He is a kind of confidence man, preying on people's vanity, ignorance, or loneliness, gaining their trust and betraying them without remorse. Like the credulous widow who wakes up one day to find the charming young man and all her savings gone, so the consenting subject of a piece of nonfiction writing learns—when the article or book appears—*his* hard lesson. Journalists justify their treachery in various ways according to their temperaments. The more pompous talk about freedom of speech and "the public's right to know"; the least talented talk about Art; the seemliest murmur about earning a living.[20]

Malcolm is probably being a little too hard on herself and her fellow journalists here—and thus hoping to appear unsullied. Nevertheless, these are remarkable disclosures. As someone who has sat for many print interviews, I can attest to the insidious way that one's vanity and trust may work to one's disadvantage. Malcolm captures the resulting derangement perfectly:

Something seems to happen to people when they meet a journalist, and what happens is exactly the opposite of what one would expect. One would think that extreme wariness and caution would be the order of the day, but in fact childish trust and impetuosity are far more common. The journalistic encounter seems to have the same regressive effect on a subject as the psychoanalytic encounter. The subject becomes a kind of child of the writer, regarding him as a permissive, all-accepting, all-forgiving mother, and expecting that the book will be written by her. Of course, the book is written by the strict, all-noticing, unforgiving father.[21]

Malcolm's fondness for Freud has not aged particularly well, but she provides an unusually candid look at how inimical a journalist's hopes often are to those of her subject.

In my experience with print journalists, the distinction between remarks being uttered on or off the record is held sacrosanct, but the distinction between truth and falsity sometimes isn't. It is instructive that the magical power of the words "this is off the record" extends only to *future* utterances; it can never be used to take one's foot out of one's mouth. This temporal asymmetry exposes the value that print journalists place on their subjects' saying something terrifically stupid. Even more insidious, calling something off the record will not keep a journalist from finding another source who can put the fact you wish to keep private *on* the record. I have had journalists ask if they could interview friends or colleagues for the (unstated) purpose of getting them to confirm a fact that I ruled out of bounds (for reasons of personal security). Apparently, this is standard operating procedure among print journalists. Having been on the receiving end of these machinations, I can say that they strike me as absolutely unethical.

I will grant, however, that the "gotcha" interview has its place—for instance, when a politician discloses opinions or habits that voters ought to be aware of. But when the point of an interview is to convey information and ideas clearly, the desire to catch a subject saying something infelicitous appears grotesque. The most inflammatory statements I have ever made are ones that I have *written* and remain willing to defend. And yet, some journalists act as though they have "caught" me saying that Islam is a terrible religion, that its core principles are degrading and idiotic, and that even in its wisest moments it isn't fit to lick the boot of Jainism. I have sometimes found that if later clarification is called for (perhaps I forgot to emphasize that I was speaking about Islam and Jainism as *doctrines*, not about Muslims and Jains as human beings), journalists may be reluctant to incorporate such nuance, while remaining steadfast in their commitment to printing the original, inflammatory statement.

One might worry that such complaints put an unfair burden on print journalism—because in radio or television interviews one doesn't get a chance to review one's remarks at all, much less amend them. But that ignores some important differences between these media. Print is the only format in which hours of conversation are regularly summarized, in whatever way a journalist finds pleasing, with just a stray quotation or two thrown in. From the subject's point of view, that allows for a frightening degree of distortion, accidental or otherwise. Compare this to television and radio, where most interviews air unedited and—whether one is given 5 minutes or 50—one is generally allowed to make as much sense as possible without later tampering. Granted, on-air interviews can be hostile, or framed by other material, but one is almost always spared the surprise of seeing oneself fundamentally misused.

Having said all this, I'm afraid I do not have a clear answer to your question. Is it necessary to give every interview subject a primer on Malcolm's thesis in advance? Probably not. But I think one has an ethical obligation to convey what one's subjects really believe, and to give them every reasonable opportunity to clarify thoughts whose first expression might be clumsy or misleading. This spirit of generosity will still allow for startling profiles and ruined careers. Having once put a foot in his mouth, many a subject will insist upon telling you why it belongs there.

6. *I'm writing from Japan, where I've lived for more than 20 years, although I was born and raised in the U.S. Here, lying is an art form. "Honne" is the Japanese term indicating what one really thinks; "tatemae," on the other hand, is the opinion or sentiment you express when the truth is inconvenient or disadvantageous. People here generally shift between the two; not doing so could easily be considered a sign of social ineptness. As you may know, Japanese ethics tend toward the situational. Also, qualities such as honesty, directness, openness, and accountability are much less valued than in the U.S. and can even mean something different. Although I agree with the principles you express in* Lying, *it isn't clear to me whether you think they could or should be applied across cultures. At least in Japan, becoming more honest wouldn't involve individuals' simply tweaking their ethics and applying themselves to the task over time; it would require turning the entire culture upside down.*

I once took a bus hoping to arrive in the city of Haldwani, in northern India. Boarding the bus, I asked the driver whether it was going to Haldwani. He assured me that it was and even sold me a ticket. After two hours, I grew concerned, because I had been told the trip wouldn't take more than one. I asked a few of my fellow passengers if we were headed to Haldwani. They assured me that we were. After another hour I realized that I was on the wrong bus. I later learned that it was considered rude in this part of India to contradict a person's stated beliefs. Apparently, these courteous people didn't want to offend me by divulging that I had boarded the wrong bus. It is difficult for me to view this cultural norm as especially conducive to human flourishing.

I can well imagine that a commitment to telling the truth might be a nonstarter in certain cultures. However, it seems to me that the way a culture treats questions of honesty and dishonesty will largely determine the psychological distance between self and other, as well as between friend and stranger. Given that intimacy, trust, and a truly global approach to ethics entail the bridging of these distances, I think universal norms regarding lying must exist. Some cultures engender more suspicion and less cooperation than others; some are more concerned about honor than about mutual understanding. Exactly how we should tune all the available dials remains an open question, but I'm prepared to say that the virtue of honesty is more than a symptom of Western provincialism. Granted, this doesn't offer much guidance for how one should function in a society where honesty isn't the norm.

7. *What about surprise parties?*

As one who has both been a recipient of a very enjoyable surprise party and attended the parties of others, I think the dishonesty occasioned by these events is probably not worth the cost. The required lies are uncomfortable to tell, and even when the event comes off without a hitch, the person being celebrated will remember that his friends and family *successfully* deceived him. That is a questionable gift. Do you really want to learn that the people you love and trust most in the world can lie to your face without your knowing? Do you really want to impart that lesson to someone else?

One can throw a "surprise" party without making the event itself a surprise: The person might be told that something has been planned but not exactly what—so he now knows not to ask. "Shut up and get in the car" might not have the same ring as "Surprise!" but it can produce many of the same pleasures. I know people who have kidnapped their spouses and taken them to the airport with bags packed. Even if the flight details can't be kept a secret, the nature of the trip can. Even if your husband knows that you are taking him to San Francisco, he will be surprised to learn that the purpose of the trip is to dive with great white sharks off the Farallon Islands.

8. *What should you do after you've already lied or withheld the truth? What if the lie was cheating on your wife? Let's say that you saw it as a mistake, and it's no longer happening: Would you recommend telling the truth? That would hurt you, your wife, your kids, the married woman you fooled around with, her husband, and her kids, and possibly end two marriages. Or should you keep it to yourself so that only you suffer (from guilt), thereby protecting everyone else?*

This is a very difficult question to answer in the abstract. One of the great benefits of committing to honesty early in life is that one doesn't stumble into situations of this kind. If you know that you cannot lie, having an extramarital affair is no longer on the menu—or, rather, to have an affair is to choose to face the consequences (most likely the end of your marriage). Nevertheless, one must begin being truthful from wherever one happens to be in life. Given a sufficiently rich history of deception, it may be hard to know how to turn over this new leaf without causing further harm.

The relevant distinction seems to be between lying and keeping a secret. Does concealing this ancient betrayal demand any ongoing deception, or is it truly buried and forgotten? If it's safely in the past, and has no implications for one's relationships in the present (apart from what would happen if the secret were known), one might argue that nothing good can come of disclosing it. However, in many cases of this kind, the maintenance of a painful secret entails a present willingness to lie that is corrosive to the relationship. I think the Golden Rule has some light to shed here: Are you concealing a secret that you would want to know about if you were the other person?

I don't see a generic answer to questions of this kind. It is possible that certain truths are best left concealed, all things considered. But if one wants to live a truly honest life, there is no substitute for having nothing to hide.

9. *Speaking as someone who has unsuccessfully applied for many jobs during the recent recession, I can say that honesty is not all it's cracked up to be. Sometimes I'm asked, "Why do you want to work here?" The honest answer might be*

"Because I'm desperate and need money" or "Because your store is close to where I live." These are guaranteed ways not to get hired, even though a person who's honest enough to admit such truths might actually be a better and more loyal employee. While dishonestly claiming that something is true might not be as good as its actually being true, it is often better than admitting that it's false. This is true in war, as you point out in the book, and it seems true in the job market. Perhaps it is true everywhere in between.

I admit that certain systems can be so corrupt, or the needs of the moment so pressing, that an honest person might find no way forward. In a job market in which everyone was successfully lying about his qualifications, a lone truth-teller might be unemployable. Given no other option but to watch his family starve, he could reasonably view his situation as morally equivalent to being at war.

But we are talking about a culture that has been poisoned by lies—and that is a culture in desperate need of changing. The situation also seems likely to correct itself, because it is in the interest of employers to know whom they are hiring. A few bad hires, and most businesses would look for better ways to assess a potential employee's qualifications (or would do a better job of checking references).

I also think you may have underestimated the power of honesty—both for winning over employers and for clarifying your own priorities. Surely you can say something positive about almost any job for which you are applying. "Why do you want to work at Starbucks?" At a minimum, you should be able to honestly say that you love coffee. If you can't, there are surely similar interviews in which you could honestly express enthusiasm for the relevant product or brand. Few employers would imagine that the job on offer is your life's calling—and if you lied and said it was, they might worry about you. Even one of the humble truths you disclosed above is a positive fact about you: "Your store is close to where I live. I won't be late for work."

10. *I believe there are situations in which a complete distortion of reality would not only be beneficial, but could actually be considered a moral responsibility. Take, for instance, the case of a loved one who is undergoing a lifesaving operation that you know has an extremely low chance of success. She asks you, "Am I going to make it?" a few hours prior to the surgery. The argument put forth in your book suggests that the best and most ethical response would be to state the truth as you know it. However, I think that the best response*

would be to indeed "deny others our view of the world" by telling your loved one that she is definitely going to be fine, which is a complete misrepresentation of your own beliefs. As you know, there is a large body of medical research that suggests the benefits of a positive disposition for recovery from illness and injury. Furthermore, even if your deception fails to increase your loved one's chances of survival (let's say the medical research is flawed on this point), I think providing consolation and confidence as opposed to fear and doubt outweighs the benefits of honesty.

I think you have ignored some aspects of these situations that make telling the truth more attractive. First is the possibility (which seems likely for someone who is not comfortable lying) that your show of confidence about the outcome of surgery will ring false. How will your loved one feel if she senses that you are lying to her out of fear? Why not say something like "Don't worry. You have a great surgeon, and I'm going to be here the whole time. If other people can get through this, you can." It seems to me that this type of reassurance addresses the needs of the moment without conveying false information. It also allows you to maintain a real connection to your loved one, rather than engaging in a dishonest and fear-based performance (however well-intentioned).

11. *The behavioral economist Dan Ariely, who as a teen-ager was seriously burned on more than 70 percent of his body, recounts a white lie that his nurses told him about a procedure he had to undergo. It was an extremely painful procedure, but they assured him that it would be painless. If he had known the truth, Ariely would have spent weeks worrying about the suffering that was to come. But because his nurses lied, he didn't begin to suffer until the procedure was actually under way. Ariely views this as a compassionate and entirely virtuous use of deception.*

Ariely is probably right about the net benefit he received from being lied to in this instance. But I doubt that misleading patients is a wise or sustainable practice. Just how many times could his nurses get away with lying to him about the painfulness of a future procedure? One can easily see how he might incur further stress after being told, truthfully, that a coming procedure would be painless—simply because he now knows that his nurses might lie. It is also possible that the truth about the original procedure could have come to him from another source. In that case, he might have spent weeks worrying both about the coming pain and about the ethical integrity of the people caring for him. Generally speaking, I think the harms of palliative lies clearly outweigh their possible benefits.

12. *I am a Chasidic Jew but no longer believe or practice privately. Should my apostasy be exposed, it would cause unimaginable suffering to my parents, siblings, and grandmother, and additional suffering for many others. It would cause my ex-wife to start a new litigation in court to change the status quo of my visitations with my children (who love me very much and are the only Chasidic people who are aware of my true beliefs), with unforeseeable consequences. The alienation and shame I would feel from my community would also be intolerable. On the one hand, I feel terrible to be living a lie, but, on the other, I don't really feel that coming out is a choice or that it would be the more ethical one if it were.*

Speaking generally, your discussion of the ethics of lying seems somewhat elitist. You appear not to consider what it might be like to live in a society where political oppression is commonplace, where hiding details about oneself can mean the difference between relative freedom and being imprisoned or killed. For instance, what about hiding one's homosexuality or doubt of God in a society where gays and atheists are routinely murdered?

Again, given a sufficiently hostile environment, lying will be the least of one's problems. If a person is likely to be killed for his beliefs, misrepresenting them would be an ethical means of self-defense. Your personal predicament also sounds very difficult, and

I can understand that the price of speaking honestly may seem too high. This is a case in which you are surrounded by people you do not trust—or, rather, whom you would trust to behave irrationally and unethically if they were to learn the truth about you. This is one of the most noxious things about religious faith and about any community based on it. Whatever its imagined virtues, faith is the enemy of open and honest inquiry. Remaining open to the powers of conversation—to new evidence and better arguments—is not only essential for rationality. It is essential for love.

ACKNOWLEDGMENTS

I am grateful for the editorial work of my wife and collaborator, Annaka Harris. The editor's job is always crucial, but with this essay my debt to Annaka is especially great, because the topic itself was her idea. In all my work, Annaka improves the content, structure, tone, and syntax—for a writer, true love takes no greater form than this . . .

I want to thank Ronald A. Howard for first teaching me about the benefits of honesty during my freshman year at Stanford and for participating in the conversation presented above.

I am indebted to my mother, whose comments improved *Lying* throughout, and to my friends Emily Elson, Tim Ferriss, and Seth Godin for their very helpful notes on an early draft of the text. I also want to thank the hundreds of readers who responded to my call for critical feedback following the publication of the first e-book edition.

Lying benefited from the expert copy editing of Martha Spaulding.

NOTES

1   Howard has put much of his material in book form: R.A. Howard and C.D. Korver, *Ethics for the Real World: Creating a Personal Code to Guide Decisions in Work and Life* (Cambridge: Harvard Business School Press, 2008). While I do not entirely agree with how the authors separate ethics from the rest of human values, I believe readers will find this a very useful book.

2   Some have argued that evolution must have selected for an ability to deceive oneself, thereby making it easier to mislead others [see William von Hippel and Robert Trivers, "The Evolution and Psychology of Self-deception," *The Behavioral and Brain Sciences* 34, no. 1 (2011): 1–16; discussion 16–56]. But whether a form of self-deception exists that is really tantamount to "lying to oneself" is still a matter of controversy. There is no question that we can be blind to facts about ourselves or about the world that we really *should* see—and the research on cognitive bias is fascinating—but the question remains whether we see the truth and unconsciously convince ourselves otherwise, or simply do not see the truth in the first place.

In any case, truly believing one's own falsehoods when in dialogue with others is tantamount to honesty. Thus, it seems that we need not worry about self-deception for the time being.

3   S. Bok, *Lying: Moral Choice in Public and Private Life* (New York: Vintage, 1999).

4   B.M. DePaulo and D.A. Kashy, "Everyday Lies in Close and Casual Relationships," *Journal of Personality and Social Psychology* 74, no.1 (Jan. 1998): 63–79.

5   B.M. DePaulo, et al., "Lying in Everyday Life," *Journal of Personality and Social Psychology* 70, no. 5 (1996): 979–995.

6   P.J. Kalbfleisch, "Deceptive Message Intent and Relational Quality," *Journal of Language and Social Psychology* 20, nos. 1–2 (2001): 214–230; T. Cole, "Lying to the One You Love: The Use of Deception in Romantic Relationships," *Journal of Social and Personal Relationships* 18, no. 1 (2001): 107–129.

7   There is a related distinction in practical ethics between negative and positive injunctions: Negative injunctions are actions we should avoid; positive injunctions are actions we should perform. The asymmetry between these two sets is impressive: We can comply with an infinite number of negative injunctions without expending any energy at all—I can abstain from killing, stealing, or vandalizing others' property without getting out of my chair. Positive injunctions, however, demand that I *do* something—raise funds for a specific

charity, for instance—and whatever I choose to do will compete with all the other ways I could use my time and attention.

Another important difference between negative and positive injunctions is that it is quite clear when one has fulfilled the former, whereas the latter are often beset by ambiguities. I can be absolutely certain I have not committed murder today. But with respect to any act of generosity, I may always wonder whether I have given enough, to the right people, in the right way, for the right purpose.

To not lie is a negative injunction, and it takes no energy to accomplish. To tell the *whole* truth, however, is a positive injunction—requiring an endless effort at communication.

8   K.A. Broomfield, E.J. Robinson, and W.P. Robinson, "Children's Understanding about White Lies," *British Journal of Developmental Psychology* 20, no. 1 (2002): 47–65.

9   At the very least, we deny them access to reality *as we see it*. Of course, when it is a matter of our *opinions*—whether we like a person's work, his new haircut, and so forth—there is no difference between the reality in question and our view of it.

10   He eventually lost twenty pounds. It has now been two years, and he has kept the weight off.

11   Many readers have pushed back strongly on this point—and some have come up with scenarios where the consequences of telling the truth are so grave, and the benefits so obscure, that the virtue of a white lie seems undeniable. For instance:

Imagine that you are with your daughter on her wedding day and are now seeing her wedding dress for the first time. Should she look fat in it, there is no way for her to put your candor to good use. You are about to walk her down the aisle; delivering anything but pure reassurance at this point seems a failure of love. This is one of the most important days in your daughter's life. You have a choice between (selfishly) maintaining your unblemished record of honesty and protecting her from feeling terrible about herself at the precise moment when she can least afford it. What do you do? Here's a hint: A good father would not say, "Yes, you look fat in that dress," and then offer advice on diet and exercise as he led his daughter down the aisle.

I agree. I suspect, however, that honest reassurance would still be possible even here. Given a father's love for his daughter, "You look beautiful"—a statement that focuses on the daughter rather than the particulars of her dress—seems like a more important truth that can be easily told. But I am not dogmatically adhering to the principle of honesty at any cost. If the parameters of the situation are tuned so that there is really no conceivable benefit to telling the truth, and the harm seems obvious, then the lie seems genuinely "white."

12 Bok (1999) makes the same point.

13 B.J. Sagarin, K. Rhoads, and R.B. Cialdini, "Deceiver's Distrust: Denigration as a Consequence of Undiscovered Deception," *Personality and Social Psychology Bulletin* 24, no. 11 (1998): 1167–1176.

14 http://www.ted.com/talks/ben_goldacre_battling_bad_science.html

15 Certain controversies arise because expert opinion has come down on both sides of an important issue. Some questions are genuinely unsettled. But confusion spreads unnecessarily whenever people in positions of power are caught lying or concealing their conflicts of interest.

16 http://healthland.time.com/2011/01/06/study-linking-vaccines-to-autism-is-fraudulent/http://www.cnn.com/2011/HEALTH/01/05/autism.vaccines/index.html

17 Several readers have pointed out that not all conspiracy theorists are liars—in fact, most are entirely sincere in their beliefs. This is probably true. But there is also no question that many conspiracy theories get their start as lies. Who, for instance, was the first to say that "four thousand Jews didn't show up to work at the World Trade Center on September 11th, 2001"? This person surely knew that he was lying. And the resulting belief in a Jewish conspiracy continues to poison minds throughout the Muslim world.

18 http://www.samharris.org/blog/item/the-riddle-of-the-gun

19 One reader informs me that the lie Howard describes here would, in fact, be a civil tort if deliberate and the other person "reasonably relies on the information to his detriment." In any case, nothing of importance in Howard's subsequent remarks hinges on the distinction.

20 J. Malcolm. 1990. *The Journalist and the Murderer.* (New York: Vintage, 1990), p. 3.

21 Ibid. p. 32.

ABOUT THE AUTHOR

Sam Harris is the author of the *New York Times* best sellers *The End of Faith*, *Letter to a Christian Nation*, *The Moral Landscape*, and *Free Will*. *The End of Faith* won the 2005 PEN Award for Nonfiction.

Mr. Harris's writing has been published in more than fifteen languages. He and his work have been discussed in *The New York Times*, *TIME*, *Newsweek*, *Scientific American*, *Nature*, *Rolling Stone*, and many other journals. His writing has appeared in *The New York Times*, *The Los Angeles Times*, *The Economist*, *Newsweek*, *The Times* (London), *The Boston Globe*, *The Atlantic*, *The Annals of Neurology*, and elsewhere.

Mr. Harris is a cofounder and the CEO of Project Reason, a nonprofit foundation devoted to spreading scientific knowledge and secular values in society. He received a degree in philosophy from Stanford University and a Ph.D. in neuroscience from UCLA. Visit his blog at www.samharris.org.

A NOTE ON THE TYPE

This book was set in Minion, a typeface designed in 1990 by Robert Slimbach for Adobe Systems, Inc. Minion combines the characteristics of late-Renaissance typefaces with the full complement of weights required for modern typesetting.

Printed and bound by Versa Press Inc,
1465 Spring Bay Road East Peoria, IL 61611.

Layout and jacket design by Neuwirth & Associates, Inc.

Cover by David Drummond, Salamander Hill Design.